100

THINGS TO DO IN
BEND, OREGON
BEFORE YOU
DIE

100

THINGS TO DO IN
BEND, OREGON
BEFORE YOU
DIE

• •

JOSHUA SAVAGE

REEDY PRESS

Library of Congress Control Number: 2019936718

ISBN: 9781681062280

Design by Jill Halpin

Photos by author unless otherwise noted.

Printed in the United States of America
19 20 21 22 23   5 4 3 2 1

Please note that websites, phone numbers, addresses, and company names are subject to change or cancellation. We did our best to relay the most accurate information available, but due to circumstances beyond our control, please do not hold us liable for misinformation. When exploring new destinations, please do your homework before you go.

DEDICATION

To my daughters and wife whom I adore and cherish.
I am grateful for all of our travels together.
May they continue to strengthen our bond, our resolve,
and our adventurous spirits.

CONTENTS

• •

Music and Entertainment

• •

Sports and Recreation

● ●

Shopping and Fashion

• •

PREFACE

Bend, Oregon, is one of the fastest growing areas in the United States for a reason. For many years it remained a small mill town on the Deschutes River, not easily accessible or known to many for its natural wonder. Fast forward to the present. The city is now a mecca for outdoor enthusiasts, beer connoisseurs, foodies, and anyone else who appreciates spectacular landscapes, fun, and adventure. Rated on countless 'best of' lists, Bend is about as awesome and amazing as a city can get, and thus far, to add to its allure, it retains a small-town feel.

When I first visited Bend I instantly fell in love with the city. The moment I stepped out of the car the smell of juniper trees and ponderosa pines filled the crisp, fresh air. Seeing the snowcapped Cascade Mountains in the backdrop I suddenly felt like the weary traveler who had been searching for Shangri-La and found it. Although my family had no plans to stay permanently, here we are now, proud residents of Bend.

Every day I love the area more. Most people are civil, friendly, and respect nature and each other. "Be nice. You're in Bend," is a local slogan that carries weight. Probably the time spent in the outdoors is what makes almost everyone happy. For this reason, the book contains more outside activities than anything else. When a place has mostly sunny days during the year and you can get back to nature within minutes, how can it not be?

• •

Other areas of Central Oregon include Redmond, La Pine, Sunriver, Sisters, Madras, and even a bit beyond Deschutes, Crook, and Jefferson Counties, but Bend is the most popular hub of the area. This part of Oregon shares a climate and a vibe that create a heavenly destination worthy of any traveler's bucket list.

100 Things to Do in Bend before You Die was easy to write because there is so much to discover in the Central Oregon region. The tougher part was choosing only 100 activities in a place where literally everyone wants to live or at least visit. Opinions may differ, but I chose based on conversations with longtime locals, devoted tourists, and of course, my own experiences. Will you agree with my choices? Read carefully and try to fully experience each activity yourself to decide, and do not be surprised to see a second book in the near future.

By writing this book my hope is that others will discover and enjoy one of the most wonderous places on Earth: Central Oregon. Please get in touch to share your opinions about the book and suggest ideas for future destinations within this amazing part of the country.

Email: ultimatescavenger@yahoo.com

You can also find me on Instagram & Facebook @ultimatescavenger

• •

TAKE THE BEND PLEDGE

As mentioned in the preface, Bend is a special place. People here respect each other and their surroundings. In fact, @VisitBend has created a pledge that encourages all locals and visitors to equally share responsibility and help to ensure Bend stays special for years to come. Please take the time to read and respect the pledge.

1. I vow to be a respectful guest in Bend's indoor and outdoor spaces.
2. I'll make my own memories, but not my own trails.
3. I will be responsible with fire during dry summer months and with ice on slick winter roads.
4. I won't risk life or limb (human or sapling) for more likes.
5. I'll be friendly and courteous, because that's the Bend way.
6. If I can't find a parking spot, I will not invent my own.
7. When playing outside, I'll prepare for shifts in weather and random episodes of magic.
8. I'll pack in reusable containers and pack out all my trash.
9. I will use my turn signal often and my car horn seldom.
10. I promise to leave Bend better than I found it.

FOOD AND DRINK

BECOME A BEER AFICIONADO
IN BEND

Stouts, IPAs, Pilsners, Ales, oh my! So many choices! Beer is a way of life in Bend. Ever visited a hop spa? Tried beer yoga? Participated in a beer relay race? Somehow, locals have managed to integrate the tasty beverage into almost every aspect of life imaginable. With over 20 breweries and counting, the town boasts some of the best brews in the entire country and takes the lead when it comes to creating new ways to enjoy beer. There seems to be a festival every other weekend to celebrate the amber nectar: Bend Brewfest, Oktoberfest, Fermentation Celebration, High Gravity Extravaganza, and many more. If you don't have a favorite type of beer, you will by the time you finish visiting the many breweries or attending the festivals! A few favorites are sprinkled throughout the book.

Visit Bend, 750 NW Lava Rd., Ste. 160
(541) 382-8048, visitbend.com/bend-ale-trail

TIP

Stop at Visit Bend and grab a free passport for the Bend Ale Trail. Make your way to at least 10 of the 18 breweries listed on the trail (no time limit required) and get your passport stamped at each location. Drinking a beer at each brewery is not required (designated drivers can claim a prize as well), but why miss out on the fun!? When you are done, return to Visit Bend and show your stamps to get a well-deserved prize (and bragging rights)!

Want to know anything else about Central Oregon? Be sure to ask the knowledgeable crew at the visitor's center while you're there. If they don't know, they will find out. Visit Bend is the perfect starting point for any trip in the area.

RELISH SOME GROWN-UP TIME
AT VELVET

Need some grown-up time away from the young ones? Find a sitter or leave the kids with the grandparents. What you need is an evening at Velvet. Grab a bite to eat downstairs, then go upstairs to a sort of speakeasy to try a drink or a few. The dimly lit setting, replete with couches, is the perfect place to kick back and relax over arguably the best cocktails in Bend. They have their own take on many 'speakeasy style' drinks, and even find a way to infuse the South American-style yerba mate into delectable concoctions worth a taste. The Mojito la Argentina is second only to those in Cuba. The blueberries in the Blue Velvet are deliciously intoxicating. Since Velvet doesn't open until 5 p.m., expect them to stay open late, often providing chill live music, intriguing people-watching, and some of the best nightlife in Bend.

805 NW Wall St.
(541) 728-0303, velvetbend.com

TRY EVERYTHING ON THE MENU
AT PLANKER SANDWICHES

Okay, it may be difficult to try everything on the menu at Planker Sandwiches, but most likely you will go back time and time again. Then, you may be tempted to get the same menu item as last time because it was so delicious, but deep down you really want to try something else. The best suggestion? Bring a group of people, have everyone order a different item, and share. More than a sandwich shop, Planker has paninis, burgers, salads, and soups. Even breakfast is available all day. Agreeable portions and fresh ingredients make the shop the 'go-to' place for a consistently satisfying meal. My personal favorite is the Italian. Once you've eaten a Planker sandwich, Subway will never measure up.

824 NW Wall St.
(541) 317-5717, plankersandwiches.com

TOUR
A CHOCOLATE FACTORY
AT GOODY'S

With local love and intention, the employees at Goody's consistently create delicious sweets. The factory store gives you a chance to see exactly how they do it. Simply visit Monday through Friday any time between 11 a.m. and 3:30 p.m. and take a free self-guided tour. On some days, especially near holidays, you may see the entire staff hard at work making truffles, ice cream, popcorn, and other sweet treats. Other days may be slower, but you can still see the machines used during the candy-making process and smell the thick aroma of sweetness in the air. While on the tour, read the detailed explanations and fun facts about how each type of candy is made. Be sure to get a free sample on the way out, and if your sweet tooth hasn't been fully satisfied, pick up a few more treats in the store before you leave.

1111 SE Division St.
(541) 385-7085, goodyschocolates.com

HANG OUT
AT ON TAP BEND

On Tap sits amid office buildings and near the busy St. Charles Hospital. It can be easily overlooked when driving by, but luckily this food truck haven has built a reputation as a great spot to hang out and fill up on some of the best grub in town. Six food trucks can usually be found open in the lot, so you can expect local and popular favorites. For beverages, On Tap beer garden has a huge selection of rotating taps and an enclosed covered patio if you prefer indoor seating. Unless it's super cold outside, I'm all about playing cornhole or sitting near the large outdoor fire pit and listening to the live bands that frequently play. If it ever gets too crowded or cold for your taste, Jackson's Corner, a few hundred feet down the road, has warm indoor seating and some of the best sandwiches and salads in Bend; definitely worth a try.

On Tap Bend, 1424 NE Cushing Dr.
ontapbend.com

Jackson's Corner, 1500 NE Cushing Dr.
(541) 382-1751, jacksonscornerbend.com

SATISFY YOUR SWEET TOOTH
AT CRAVIN'S

This place stocks so much candy that there is barely room to walk around inside of this sweet-lover's heaven! Neither kids nor adults can pass by Cravin's Candy Emporium without lingering at the window and begging to go inside. Treat the kids (and yourself) to the many colors that jump out as you are surrounded by every candy imaginable. A library card catalog filled with different types of gum, PEZ dispensers of all the favorite characters, a wall full of sour candy, giant jellybeans, root beer barrels, gelato, gummies of all kinds, orange slices, cotton candy, popcorn, toys, games; I think you get the point. There is something at Cravin's for everyone. In the back of the store the original *Willy Wonka* movie continually plays on a large flatscreen. What's really cool is that many of the cast members (including Charlie and Willy Wonka) have actually visited the store and have pics with their autographs on the wall. Probably no other place in Oregon has so many different types of candy!

818 NW Wall St.
(541) 617-9866, cravinscandy.com

DO YOUR BEST JACK NICHOLSON IMPRESSION
AT WORTHY BREWING

A first visit to Worthy Brewing might make one curious as to why memorabilia featuring Jack Nicholson and the author Ken Kesey are scattered throughout the building. The reason? The Douglas fir bar tops, tabletops, and benches may look like ordinary wood, but it was sourced from the Oregon Mental Hospital where the 1975 Oscar-winning *One Flew Over the Cuckoo's Nest* was filmed. If this alone isn't enough to inspire a visit, the brewery has no shortage of delicious food. The menu suggests excellent beer and food pairings which are carefully chosen by the chef. Try the pizza, made with fresh herbs straight from the brewery's own greenhouse. Worthy also leads the way in beer innovation. In fact, the owner, in conjunction with Oregon State University, created the now-popular Strata hop used in many beers across the country. Worthy's Strata IPA beer is a Bend favorite (and mine)!

495 NE Bellevue Dr.
(541) 639-4776, worthybrewing.com

ENTER THE WORLD OF COLD BREW COFFEE
AT RIFF TAPROOM

Riff, the world's first cold brew coffee taproom, recently opened in Bend. In case you're wondering, cold brewed coffee isn't iced coffee. It refers to the way the coffee grounds are steeped in water for a long period of time, usually twelve to twenty-four hours. Although fascinating, I'll spare you more details, but cold brewing does have an effect on the taste, and in a favorable way. Try a flight with different coffees to see what I mean. Much more than coffee, Riff serves local beers (and even collaborates with the local breweries to create new types of beverages), kombucha (a local favorite), and other drinks. They serve food as well, but not the pastries you are used to in most coffee shops. The cheese and charcuterie (meat) plates are amazing, especially the Manchego. In fact, the owners must have exceptional palates, because the garnishes and other items that accompany the plates are perfectly paired. The Pacific Northwest has a wide variety of amazing coffee shops, but at Riff, you are witnessing the evolution of the drink.

555 Arizona Ave., Ste. 30
(541) 312-9330, riffcoldbrewed.com

IMAGINE A TRIP TO ITALY
AT BONTÀ

Why bother with a trip to Italy when you can experience the world's best gelato right here in Bend? No joke, Bontà Natural Artisan Gelato makes some of the best handcrafted gelato I have ever tasted, and believe me, with two daughters who love ice cream, I have tried quite a lot. After a yearlong trip around the world, the owners, Jeff and Julie, wanted to capture the exotic flavors they encountered and bring them back to Bend. They then studied under two Italian gelato masters to hone their skills. Now, using ingredients from both local farms and producers, they make everything from scratch and continually tweak their own unique recipes. Flavors like Tumalo Lavender & Honey, Strawberry Rhubarb, and Thump Espresso can't be found anywhere else. My personal favorite is the Dulce de Leche & Sea Salt but try as many flavors as you like and hear the story behind them before deciding which is your favorite. Once you taste the gelato here, you will never be satisfied with store-bought ice cream again.

920 NW Bond St., Ste. 108
(541) 306-6606, bontagelato.com

SIP A BREW
WITH A SWEET VIEW
AT BEND BREWING COMPANY

Of all the breweries in town Bend Brewing Company boasts perhaps the most enviable location. The second-oldest brewery in Bend has one of the sweetest views of the Deschutes River where it meets Mirror Pond. Super family-friendly, you can dine, drink, or play cornhole in the large courtyard overlooking the water or keep warm near the long, heated, outdoor fire pit during the cold weather. In fact, BBC has deep roots in the community and makes ample use of the courtyard year round with events like Yoga on the Pond, Rhythm and Brews, and other fun activities you may not associate with typical breweries. Sports fans will also be delighted to catch their favorite games on all the big screens inside. The owners and staff at BBC have given serious thought to providing something for everyone to enjoy, resulting in an all-in-one place to hang out and have fun.

1019 NW Brooks St.
(541) 383-1599, bendbrewingco.com

BEWARE
LOS LUCHADORES
AT BARRIO

In this food truck-gone-restaurant, images of Mexican wrestlers (los luchadores) adorn the walls. More than Mexican food, Barrio offers some of the best and most unique Latin cuisine in Central Oregon. The paella with chorizo and chicken is incredible, probably the best I have tasted outside of Spain, and there are a few other varieties to try. The several types of tacos will raise the bar for what you will accept as a taco. If you have a large family or group of friends, order several dishes to share. If it's just you and a friend, stop by during happy hour and load up on tacos and margaritas. Barrio's cocktails, like la Tigre, are of a type and quality I have never seen anywhere else. And for those needing a fix on the other side of town, Barrio still keeps its famous food truck rolling, but there are a lot more choices at the restaurant. In either place, you cannot go wrong with whatever you order.

915 NW Wall St.
(541) 389-2025, barriobend.com

AWAKEN YOUR APPETITE
AT SPARROW BAKERY

From the outside it's hard to imagine this small, rustic-looking brick building could hold much.

Walk inside and Sparrow Bakery is bustling and lively with the tantalizing aromas of freshly baked breads and pastries. Culinary master bakers mix all the right herbs and spices to satisfy your cravings first thing in the morning. Order a slice of carrot cake or banana bread that is so moist it will melt in your mouth. Try the Bendfamous Ocean Roll, a croissant roll made with cardamom, sugar, and vanilla. If you have a larger appetite for breakfast or brunch, Sparrow has several signature sandwiches and soups. The perfect start to a day, the bakery has become so admired that you can find their goodies all over in town, especially in coffee shops.

50 SE Scott St.
(541) 330-6321, thesparrowbakery.net

PLEASE YOUR PALATE
AT DRAKE

When first walking into Drake you get the look and feel of a retro diner. But stay awhile, view the menu, and the atmosphere of this downtown restaurant begins to feel more upscale. The waiter or waitress will greet you with a bag of the house popcorn, full of flavor and whetting your appetite. Since the restaurant always finds ways to be innovative and add to the menu, you may want to try the daily special or ask for a seasonal dish. My personal favorite, a mainstay on the menu, is the mac and cheese made with white and yellow cheddar. It pops with flavor and is perfect with a local IPA. For lunch or dinner Drake is a great choice--right in the heart of everything, and a good way to begin or end a trip downtown.

801 NW Wall St.
(541) 306-3366, drakebend.com

TASTE TEST ALL WEEKEND
AT THE BITE OF BEND

The Bite of Bend might be the largest taste test that takes place in Oregon. Held on a weekend during the middle of June, several downtown streets are closed, the weather this time of year perfect, and many local restaurants and food carts set up shop to share their goodies with the large crowds. For a buck or two a bite, you can try agreeable portions of Central Oregon's yummiest food. A few friendly competitions take place over the weekend as well. While the kids compete in the root beer run and make root beer floats, the adults can sign up for the beer run. Top local chefs also have a competition where they get a black box of ingredients and have to create a dish on the fly. During the mixology showcase local distilleries celebrate the creation of unique cocktails. My goal in life—to be a judge!

Downtown Bend
(541) 323-0964, biteofbend.com

INDULGE IN HAPPY HOUR
AT THE ICONIC PINE TAVERN

The most iconic restaurant in Bend has something you don't see every day in a dining room; two giant ponderosa pines growing through the roof! Over its eighty years in business, the Pine Tavern has gained a reputation as a must-visit destination in Bend for a number of reasons. The food is exceptional, the view overlooking Mirror Pond is breathtaking, and the bar was recently voted the best happy hour in Bend. Over the years Pine Tavern has evolved to keep pace with the times, and the establishment looks like it will be around for another eighty years. Be sure to try the sourdough scones with honey butter.

967 NW Brooks St.
(541) 382-5581, pinetavern.com

ABSORB THE SUNSET
AT CRUX FERMENTATION

Imagine a panoramic view of the sun setting behind the Cascade Mountains in a large, comfortable courtyard. The kids are playing. You are surrounded by friends or family. No need to cook or clean up, yet you have a wide variety of food and drink available. Sound too good to be true? At Crux Fermentation Project dreams become reality. The brewery has a taproom with a seemingly endless supply of unique brews and a food menu that promises to please. And just to give us more choices, the courtyard has food carts set up as well. For a little extra love and to make the sunset even more magical, every day Crux celebrates the 'Sundowner Hour' with discounts on food and drink. Dreams really do come true.

50 SW Division St.
(541) 385-3333, cruxfermentation.com

EAT LOCAL
WITH CENTRAL OREGON LOCAVORE

The folks at Central Oregon Locavore know how to have a good time. Promoting the farm-to-table lifestyle, their goal is to raise awareness about eating locally, healthily, and sustainably. Not a restaurant, but more than a grocery store, Locavore brings about this awareness in the most entertaining way possible. Local chefs, restaurants, and farms collaborate to offer food-related classes and events. Why not learn a Bollywood dance while trying a delicious feast of Indian cuisine? Surely you have been wanting to learn how to make handmade tortillas from the chefs at the local Mexican restaurant? Have you ever met and eaten with the farmer of the savory meal you are enjoying? Seriously, after learning about this place, I feel I can become a culinary master. More importantly, I am getting schooled on the importance of eating locally. If you can't attend one of the events, stop by the marketplace and pick up some fresh, locally raised and/or grown food.

1841 NE 3rd St.
(541) 633-7388, centraloregonlocavore.org

FINE DINE FROM A TO Z
IN BEND

Whether they know it or not, two restaurants seem to be in constant competition with each other to win over local palates in Bend: Ariana and Zydeco. Both have exquisite dishes, so it really depends on your taste and your mood. Why not enjoy both? Zydeco Kitchen & Cocktails is where the Pacific Northwest meets the South. Not many places offer tasty Baby Back Ribs and Redfish on the same menu. Ariana has its own take on the Pacific Northwest and fuses it with a Mediterranean style. Indulge yourself with the Chef's Tasting Menu, a five-course tour that will leave you blissfully satisfied. No two restaurants are alike, and you cannot go wrong with either of these. Be sure to try both, just not on the same night.

Ariana, 1304 NW Galveston Ave.
(541) 330-5539, arianarestaurantbend.com

Zydeco Kitchen & Cocktails, 919 NW Bond St.
(541) 312-2899, zydecokitchen.com

FILL UP
ON A TASTY PIZZA PIE
AT PIZZA MONDO

I could live on pizza, and as a delivery driver during college, I basically did. So, in my opinion, no city list is complete without a good pizza place on it. In Bend, Pizza Mondo tops the list of delectable pizza pies, and I'm not the only one who thinks so. Locals have voted it the 'Best Pizza' for an unprecedented 21 years in a row! Whatever suits you, chances are this pizzeria will satisfy your palate and keep you coming back for more. Meat lover? Try the Big Island or Pork-A-Palooza. Prefer the vegetarian option? Get the Mount Olympus. Or hey, just drop by to grab a slice. Pizza Mondo is the perfect family-friendly spot to fill up while exploring downtown. Don't feel like getting out? Sit on the couch and make a phone call. They deliver! I'm getting hungry just writing this. Gotta go!

811 NW Wall St.
(541) 330-9093, pizzamondobend.com

TREAT YOURSELF TO AN EARLY MORNING DRINK
AT MCKAY COTTAGE RESTAURANT

Tradition says it's never too early to drink a Bloody Mary or mimosa. Some people would even argue it's a healthy way to start the day. I mean, the drinks do have fruit juice and all, right? McKay Cottage restaurant is known as the hot spot for breakfast in Bend, and not only because of the morning libations. Open from 7 a.m. to 2 p.m., McKay's menu full of favorites like the Gourmet Breakfast Sandwich and Oatmeal Pancakes provides the perfect comfort food all day long. Mornings can often be a bit chilly around town, but the staff at McKay's Cottage will offer you blankets if you decide to sit outside. Some tables have fire pits to keep you warm. After your belly is full you may choose to go across the street to Sawyer Park for a quiet walk along the river. Start your day off right at McKay's.

62910 O.B. Riley Rd.
(541) 383-2697, themckaycottage.com

JOIN
THE KOMBUCHA CRAZE

After reading this far you probably think that beer is the only beverage in Bend. Not so. Rapidly gaining popularity is kombucha, sometimes called the nectar of the gods. A type of fermented tea, many people enjoy the taste, while others point to the health benefits. Either way, if you haven't tried the drink before, a world of new flavors awaits, from sweet Coconut Lime to spicy Lemon Ginger. Stores around the country carry kombucha but here in Bend local restaurants have it on tap. And if you want to go straight to the source where it's freshest, stop at the Humm Kombucha Taproom, one of the largest, most innovative brewers in the country. Here you can mix and match and try as many flavors as you like. You may end up with a new favorite drink.

Humm Kombucha, 1125 NE 2nd St.
(541) 306-6329, hummkombucha.com

GET A HOPPY EDUCATION
ON A DESCHUTES BREWERY TOUR

Deschutes Brewery holds the title as the oldest brewery in town, and it is also one of the largest craft breweries in the country. Their production facility on the Deschutes River is ginormous and on windy days when they are brewing, the smell the hops permeates the air for miles. Lucky for you, the facility offers tours seven days a week. Before the tour starts, the guide offers a free, cold, canned beverage. Then, in a little less than an hour, you will make your way through halls of hops, giant steel vats full of wort, futuristic looking bottling machines, and every other step of the beer making process. By then, your beer will probably be gone and you'll want to try one of the other types the tour guide mentioned. Mosey on down to the taproom, taste as many as you like, and order a favorite.

901 SW Simpson Ave.
(541) 385-8606, deschutesbrewery.com/brewery-tour

TOWER

TOWER
MOUNTAINFILM ON TOUR
FEB 22 · 23 A FUNDRAISER FOR

Photo courtesy of Toni Toreno
@BendPhotoTours

MUSIC AND ENTERTAINMENT

SEE A LIVE SHOW
AT LES SCHWAB AMPHITHEATER

During the summer months the big names come to Bend: Dave Matthews, Michael Franti, the Pixies, and Steve Miller to name a few. The Les Schwab Amphitheater is hands down the best place to see live music in the city. And it's not just the bands. Blue skies slowly giving way to the sunset, the background whoosh of running water from the nearby Deschutes River, a large open grass space without conventional seating, and an energized crowd all collude to create an electric atmosphere. Even if you cannot attend a show, the sound and enthusiasm carry across much of the city, and you can hear the music clearly almost anywhere nearby. When performers aren't on stage the amphitheater still hosts festivals and other events. Even during the winter, the grass area is open for all to enjoy, including the hundreds (maybe thousands) of Canadian geese that flock to the area.

344 SW Shevlin Hixon Dr.
(541) 318-5457, bendconcerts.com

TIP

When the holiday season arrives, Santa Claus flies to Bend by helicopter! He uses the open grass field at Les Schwab Amphitheater as a landing pad. Rain, shine, or heavy snow, it's a sight to see. Be sure to take the kids, who usually rush him after he steps out and starts passing out candy and hugs.

SING YOUR HEART OUT
DURING KARAOKE AT ASTRO LOUNGE

At night, when the downtown streets seem empty and every place in Bend looks closed, stop by the Astro Lounge which will still be open and kicking. If you are feeling extra frisky, take the stage on a Thursday karaoke night to sing a favorite song. Get cheers from the crowd and feel like a star. Perhaps you will be asked to sign autographs afterwards. On other nights the lounge is hopping with live music of every genre, open mic, bingo, and other late-night entertainment. Be sure to order a mixed drink because the bartenders pride themselves on creating amazing cocktails. It's almost as fun to watch these skilled mixologists as it is to sip the drinks!

939 NW Bond St.
(541) 388-0116, astroloungebend.com

TEST YOUR ENDURANCE
AT BEND WINTERFEST

Oregonians are a hardy breed, and no matter the weather, they know how to party! In fact, they throw a huge three-day festival on some of the coldest days of the year. WinterFest, held in mid-February in the Old Mill District, celebrates a time of year when most people prefer to be inside next to a cozy fireplace. Not in Bend! Like most festivals, plenty of food and drink tents are available. Kids' activities and local vendors are abundant. Musicians play throughout the weekend and you can't miss the dog shows. But what really sets Winterfest apart from other festivals are the friendly competitions. Seeing the intricately carved ice sculptures is alone worth the price of admission. The custom-built fire pits not only keep you warm, but they are truly works of art, especially when they come alive at dark. With so much entertainment you may even forget how cold it is outside!

Old Mill District
(541) 323-0964, oregonwinterfest.com

BECOME A TRUE FILM BUFF
AT BENDFILM FESTIVAL

The Avengers, *Star Wars*, *Wedding Crashers*—those movies are good and all, but most of the best films being created are independent. Rated the best film festival in the Pacific Northwest, the annual BendFilm Festival gives you an opportunity to see some of these high quality indie films. More intimate than commercial film fests, BendFilm is four days during the fall when you will get the chance to meet and engage the actors, directors, and others involved in the movie, not to mention four days' worth of parties! Growing bigger each year, the most recent festival featured nine screens in Central Oregon showcasing films from around the world. If you stick to the big, cookie-cutter, blockbuster movies, you really can't consider yourself a movie buff, but after attending this festival you will have a fresh perspective and appreciation for quality film.

1000 NW Wall St., Ste. 240
(541) 388-FEST, bendfilm.org

TIP

Have a future moviemaker in the family? BendFilm is deeply involved in the community. The BendFilm Future Filmmakers competition gives kids in 5th through 12th grades the opportunity to hone their talents and learn their craft better. Prizes are awarded and more importantly, kids get to interact with other filmmakers and get recognized.

DISPLAY THOSE HIDDEN TALENTS
DURING OPEN MIC NIGHT

Talent overflows on Tuesday evenings at the Crow's Feet Commons. Musicians, poets, and storytellers of all backgrounds descend upon the oldest building in Bend to share their skills with those willing to watch and listen. Grab a coffee, a beer, or other beverage and a light snack while enjoying the carefully crafted lyrics and melodies of those brave enough to get in front of an audience. The open mic nights prove that people do not have to be famous to be talented and inspirational, and quite possibly, you are watching a future superstar. If you are feeling courageous enough, feel free to share your own talents. Performers of all ages are welcome, and the engaged audience is always encouraging.

875 NW Brooks St.
(541) 323-3955, thecommonsbend.com

CATCH A PERFORMANCE
AT TOWER THEATRE

You would never guess that the iconic Tower Theatre began as a cafeteria opened by the same ladies who went on to create the Pine Tavern (#15). Over the years the building has changed hands often and even been closed down a few times. But now, thanks to a caring community, the large bright neon lights make the venue one of Bend's most prized and recognizable destinations. The theatre has been beautifully renovated to create an amazingly intimate and comfortable experience for the performers and their audiences. As host to 220-plus activities a year, you can bet there is something for everyone—Celtic, rock, mariachi concerts, musicals and plays, films, nature nights, weddings, presentations—the list goes on. Often called Bend's Living Room, Tower Theatre stands at the apex of the city's cultural vibe.

835 NW Wall St.
(541) 317-0700, towertheatre.org

SUPPORT A FUTURE OSCAR WINNER
AT THOROUGHLY MODERN PRODUCTIONS

For a smaller town Bend is bursting with talent, and at Thoroughly Modern Productions big talent comes in small packages. Here kids interested in stagecraft can develop new skills and follow their passions. Whether performing in front of an audience or working behind the scenes, there is a place for anyone interested in learning about theatre. Even if you don't have children, I suggest watching a production, often performed at the iconic Tower Theatre (#28). Popular versions of musicals and plays like *The Wizard of Oz*, *Annie*, *Legally Blonde*, and *Willy Wonka* will pleasantly surprise you. Plus, the courage and hard work of these kids deserve praise. I wish I had had the guts to get on stage, especially when I was their age!

63595 Boyd Acre Rd.
(541) 678-0313, thoroughlymodernprod.com

RIDE THROUGH BEND IN STYLE
WITH WHEEL FUN RENTALS

Walking to a destination can sometimes take too long and when driving you often miss the blissful surroundings. Plus, who wants to find a place to park, especially during the busy season? Biking is the best way to do Bend and Wheel Fun Rentals has everything from eight passenger Surreys to tandem bicycles, multi-speed bikes, baby joggers, and the regular two- wheeled bikes most of us are accustomed to. Go wherever you like during the rental times or take the self-guided bicycle tour. Ask for the map which gives detailed directions and brief explanations about some of the best destinations in Bend. The route passes through McKay Park, the Deschutes River Trail, Mirror Pond, and more. A few food suggestions are also included (or you could just carry along this book), but we like to pack a lunch and have a picnic in one of the parks on the route.

603 SW Mill A Drive
(541) 408-4568, wheelfunrentals.com/or/bend/old-mill-district

CHILL OUTSIDE
DURING MUNCH & MUSIC

When summer arrives in Bend, the weather is perfect, and everyone is happy and ready to spend every waking moment outside. On Thursday evenings during July and August the crowds descend on Drake Park (#61) for free music events, better known as Munch & Music. The outdoor amphitheater backs up to the river, and the sweet melodies liven up the mood making everyone ecstatic that it's finally summer. Grab yourself a low-back chair or blanket and share the grassy area with friends or complete strangers; you'll make friends soon enough. Local artisans have tents set up to sell their wares and of course there will be plenty of food trucks to appease your appetite. There may even be a bouncy house or two to wear out the kiddos.

Drake Park, 777 NW Riverside Blvd.
munchandmusic.com

FEEL THE MUSIC
AT VOLCANIC THEATRE PUB

A concert at Volcanic Theatre Pub in Bend is about as up close and personal as you can get; so much so that the music reverberates though your body. This large warehouse has the perfect amount of space for live shows, with plenty of room to dance and move around or lounge on cozy sofas, recliners, and other seating. VTP mostly hosts local and national musicians, but you'll also see an eclectic mix of other types of performances. One visit might feel like a rambunctious party and the next like a chill evening with friends. Watch a standup comedian when you need a little laughter, see a live theatre show if you're in a cerebral mood, relax and watch a movie, or just take the family and enjoy the positive vibes.

70 SW Century Dr.
(541) 323-1881, volcanictheatre.com

FOCUS ON YOUR PHOTOGRAPHY SKILLS
WITH BEND PHOTO TOURS

These days, smart phones and affordable digital cameras allow everyone the chance to snap great pics. I like to think I'm a decent photographer, but true photography is an art with many technicalities to be learned. The talented crew at Bend Photo Tours will help sharpen your skills and teach the artistic aspects of taking amazing pictures. The company offers year-round guided tours, workshops, photo talks, and personalized tutoring for the novice to the expert. Capture the Cascades by helicopter, snap Tumalo Falls while snowshoeing, or choose your own expedition. What better way to boost your abilities and learn the intricacies of photography than through hands-on adventures among the limitless beauty of Central Oregon?

We all want that perfect photo to hang on the wall or post on Instagram. After a Bend Photo Tour, it will seem all your pictures are worth framing.

550 SW Industrial Way, Ste. 105
(541) 640-1089, bendphototours.com

BURN THOSE CALORIES
ON A CYCLE PUB TOUR

Maybe you don't really feel like biking for miles or you could use some help. Maybe drinking, socializing, and casually pedaling from time to time sounds more your speed. And why feel bad about drinking that beer, or two, or three? You're on a Cycle Pub tour so the harder you pedal, the more you can drink! Cycle Pub offers rides with tour guides on non-traditional bikes from as few as four people and up to fourteen. That's a lot of horsepower! It's a fun way to see some of the main spots in Bend, and you don't necessarily have to drink alcohol to make it a family trip (12 and up). The bikes make at least one stop at Silver Moon Brewing but can also stop other places if you're running on empty and need a refill on the growler.

550 SW Industrial Way, Ste. 105
(541) 678-5051, cyclepub.com

RELIVE YOUR YOUTH
AT VECTOR VOLCANO

Heart racing, hands sweating, blood pumping; all the excitement will make you feel like a kid again at Vector Volcano. A blast from the past, I thought I had grown out of gaming until I saw the well-kept arcade games from the 80s and 90s like Pac-Man, Kung Fu Master, Galaga, Mortal Kombat, Frogger, and other favorites. The arcade has an area up front with pinball machines that take coins to play. In the same area you can purchase drinks. Beyond the front, pay by the hour and get limitless play on all the other games. Introducing the classics of my childhood to my daughters was just as much fun, and they thought I was some kind of ninja master until they saw me get beaten by another guy my age in Street Fighter II.

111 NW Oregon Ave.
vectorvolcanoarcade.com

DISCOVER
THE SECRET ROOMS
OF MCMENAMINS

McMenamins has an unconventional flavor like no other place in Bend. Once St. Francis Catholic School, the building is now home to a restaurant, a hotel, brewery, a hot pool (#37), and—don't tell anyone—secret rooms. The rooms are not difficult to find but to savor the experience of this unique establishment, first enter through the restaurant and admire the exotic art from all over the world scattered about. The spirit of St. Francis School stays alive through the artwork, photos, and other memorabilia that adorn the walls. Go outside. Across the parking lot and past the Cigar Room, head for the hotel called the Art House. Now we can search for the secret rooms (and again, don't tell anyone). On the first floor, search for a hidden entrance that takes you to a blacklight room reminiscent of *Alice in Wonderland*, a popular spot for taking deliciously eerie Snapchat pics. The hidden entrance on the second floor will lead to a room with chalkboard walls full of aphorisms, autographs, and scribbled art. Leave your mark. On the third floor search for the Broom Closet, which from the outside looks like a storage room for Quidditch broomsticks. Step inside and you have entered a small and cozy speakeasy. Time to reward yourself with a drink for finding the three mysterious secret rooms.

700 NW Bond St.
(541) 382-5174, mcmenamins.com/old-st-francis-school

REVITALIZE IN THE HOT POOL
AT MCMENAMINS

Truthfully, I could write a whole book about the wonders of McMenamins. Scattered around Washington and Oregon, each location has an eccentricity that makes it stand out. Bend, however, has a crown jewel feature that no other location can claim; a large Turkish-style hot pool. Beautifully crafted stained-glass windows depict the sun, the moon, and St. Francis's compassion for animals. The shimmering turquoise tiles give the pool an opulent air. Add the fountain, water-spouting lions, and an open ceiling and you truly feel like royalty. Open to the public for a small hourly fee, the pool provides the perfect relaxation any time, but especially on the colder winter days. Before you take a dip be sure to grab a drink at the bar and watch the snow fall as you soak! Nowhere else will you encounter such an eclectic and relaxing place.

700 NW Bond St.
(541) 382-5174, mcmenamins.com/old-st-francis-school

TIP

Do you like collecting stuff, or in
this case, experiences? McMenamins has its
own passport available. Get it stamped at each
eclectic location (over 50 around the Pacific
Northwest) and earn food, merchandise, concert
tickets, and even lodging. These places are
amazingly awesome!

IGNITE YOUR CREATIVITY
AT 9TH STREET VILLAGE

What started as the DIY Cave has quickly grown into the largest creative environment in Bend. A giant maker space, this is the ideal area to let your creative juices flow or learn new skills. Classes for all ages teach how to work with metal, wood, paint, and more. An outdoor 'tiny home build' space can be rented and allows for massive projects. Over the last few years the area has expanded to become the 9th Street Village and now includes an artist co-op (Bright Place Gallery), a skate shop (SOLSK8S), a music studio, food trucks, and of course, a brewery (Bevel Craft Brewing). Truly living up to its name as a village, everything you need is on site. When your imagination exhausts itself or needs a break, grab a drink and a snack, and mingle with other likeminded creatives.

DIYcave
444 SE 9th St., Ste. 150
(541) 388-2283, diycave.com

SOLSK8S
484 SE 9th St., Ste. 150
(541) 797-7616, seedoflifeskateboards.com

Bright Place Gallery
909 SE Armour Rd.
(541) 359-1309, brightplacegallery.com

Bevel Craft Brewing
911 SE Armour Rd., Ste. B
(541) 972-3835, bevelbeer.com

WITNESS THE 4TH OF JULY PET PARADE
BEFORE WATCHING THE FIREWORKS

Pets, especially dogs, have it made in Bend. They are treated like children, maybe better. In fact, Bend has been named one of the 'most dog friendly' cities by a number of publications. So, you can bet that on the 4th of July, the pet parade is a sight to behold. Hundreds of animals walk the streets of downtown strutting their stuff and sniffing their friends' backsides. Their owners sometimes pull them in wagons or small bikes, in baby strollers, or on elaborate floats. Some pets are all dazzled up in snazzy outfits, usually with red, white, and blue for the occasion. Mostly dogs participate, but you may also see horses, lizards, snakes, and possibly even a baby coyote or badger. Don't own a pet? Grab your favorite stuffed animal and be part of the entertainment!

Downtown Bend
bendparksandrec.org/activities/4th-of-july-festival

GET A BLAST FROM THE PAST
AT THE LAST BLOCKBUSTER

Once an empire with thousands of stores, Blockbuster Video now has one last physical location in the entire world. And yes, the city of Bend is lucky enough to claim it. The store recently celebrated its survival with a block party and has become so iconic that a local brewery, 10 Barrel, brewed a black ale beer in its name. If nostalgia is not enough reason for you to visit, Blockbuster still maintains a large selection of DVDs and Blue Rays, some obscure and hard to find online—fairly priced, I might add. In the age of On Demand and Netflix, it is fun to see my kids walk around the store and stare in awe at generations of films. With so many movies, they have trouble making a choice! It really makes me think about what we have lost that we used to take for granted. Sign up for a membership, true movie aficionados!

211 NE Revere Ave.
(541) 385-9111, blockbuster.com

CUT LOOSE
AT THE DESCHUTES COUNTY FAIR & RODEO

I'm no cowboy, but that doesn't keep me from having a good time at the Deschutes County Fair & Rodeo. The largest event in Central Oregon takes place annually for almost a full week in early August. Devour a funnel cake or cotton candy with the kids. Ride the Extreme Scream or tone it down on a carousel. Visit the prize pigs, goats, and other livestock. Listen to live concerts from both local and well-known musicians. Watch in awe as the true cowboys attempt to ride a bucking horse for eight seconds. And despite everything I mentioned, much, much more is happening. With so much entertainment to choose from, all ages and all types of people can have a blast. You don't have to be a cowboy to enjoy this ride!

3800 Southwest Airport Way, Redmond, OR
(541) 548-2711, expo.deschutes.org/fair

UNCOVER
THE BEST OF BEND
WITH THE ULTIMATE SCAVENGER

The most adventurous and exciting way to see the many treasures of Bend is on a scavenger hunt. The Ultimate Scavenger offers year-round, personalized hunts or tours for individuals, groups, and businesses. For the competitive types among us, the travel company has a huge citywide scavenger hunt once a year. Random teams with silly names are cut loose to decipher and act out clues while scouring the city in the allotted time. The first group to complete the hunt with the most points is the Ultimate Scavenger and wins cash money! Other contestants who finish the hunt win prizes as well. The hunts are a great way to test your knowledge of the city and to discover new things you never knew existed. Sign me up again!

Citywide
(901) 210-5104, facebook.com/ultimatescavenger

TIP

For those who want a souvenir or prefer
to do a scavenger hunt at their own pace,
The Ultimate Scavenger recently released
an interactive activity book. Filled with
destinations and trivia, it's an entertaining way to
learn about Bend. Plus, you get a certificate and
the opportunity to win prizes upon completion!
The book can be purchased at many local
shops or digitally on Amazon.

https://amzn.to/2XVQCQk

SPORTS AND RECREATION

LEARN TO DOWNHILL SKI OR SNOWBOARD
AT MOUNT BACHELOR

On any clear day in Bend, Mount Bachelor can be seen standing alone and rising impressively above the landscape. Not really a mountain, this volcano (no worries, it isn't expected to erupt anytime soon) is a winter wonderland for skiing and snowboarding enthusiasts during the snowy months of the year. For beginners like me, it's a chance to learn the difference between downhill and Nordic skiing, and to find out if snowboarding is as gnarly as it looks. I suggest newbies purchase the SKI OR RIDE IN 5 pass which gets you five lessons based on your own schedule from seasoned instructors. Tickets for the lift and the equipment are included as well but bring your own warm clothing!

13000 SW Century Dr.
(541) 382-1709, mtbachelor.com

LEARN A NEW SKILL
OR IMPROVE AN EXISTING ONE

Bend's Parks & Recreation runs such well-developed, well-orchestrated city-wide programming that other cities should take note. Besides keeping the numerous parks around town immaculately clean and landscaped, they offer many recreational opportunities to the community. Camps, after-school programs, recreational activities, tours, and year-round classes are available for every age group. Want to take martial arts? Learn how to snow ski? Build a robot? Paint? Take a trip abroad? Whatever your interest, you will almost certainly find a class to guide you in the right direction. Bend is a tight-knit community, and Bend Parks & Recreation is the glue that keeps it together and thriving.

(541) 389-7275, bendparksandrec.org/activities

LOSE YOURSELF IN THE FOREST
AT SHEVLIN PARK

Not many cities have a natural recreation area the size of Shevlin Park. At almost one thousand acres, the area is an ideal way to escape city life and rejuvenate in the forest. A small pond near the parking lot is perfect for beginning fishermen or those who want to relax. Tumalo Creek rambles lazily through the park, and most of the trails follow it closely, allowing hikers to stop and listen to the peaceful, flowing water. Have a picnic or take a dip. And while many trails near Bend are covered in snow during the winter months, those at Shevlin Park are usually still accessible. The quaking aspens, ponderosa pines, and other native trees and plants are beautiful year-round and offer a sense of remoteness that lets you think you are far away from civilization. You may never want to leave.

18920 Northwest Shevlin Park Rd.
bendparksandrec.org/park/shevlin-park

TIP

Sign the kids up for Cougar Camp during the summer! The best day camp in the area, it's a great way for children to explore the forest, meet new friends, and get interested in the outdoors.

BOND WITH NATURE
ON THE DESCHUTES RIVER TRAIL

The Deschutes River Trail is the experience that first made me fall in love with Bend. Easily accessible from many points around town, within seconds you can hear the peaceful flow of the river, be surrounded by massive boulders, and smell the sweet scent of pines, juniper, and other vegetation. The well-traveled trail hugs the river to create a large loop and the city is continually finding ways to expand and improve it. Interpretive signs educate hikers about local vegetation, wildlife, and the history of the area. There are plenty of spots to stop and rest or take in the scenery. Perfect for walking or running, the trail is also excellent for getting kids interested in hiking. One of about eight possible access points, Farewell Bend Park is my favorite place to begin.

bendtrails.org/trail/deschutes-river-trail

TIP

Naturally, kids enjoy hiking more when they are having fun. To get them interested in the outdoors and hiking, play games along the trail. Create a scavenger hunt, deputize them rangers, or let them stop along the way to explore. We all know that fairies live in the forest, and my daughters like to search for hidden fairy holes and build houses for the hard-to-spot creatures from whatever they find lying around in the forest. Their imaginations run wild!

DIG FOR TREASURE
NEAR BEND

Grab the shovels, goggles, picks, gloves, and whatever other digging tools you have at home and go rockhounding! It's completely legal in many areas of the state to collect rocks like obsidian, agate, petrified wood, and Oregon's state rock—the Thunderegg. For the beginner, Richardson's Rock Ranch in nearby Madras is the best place to start. They suggest which areas are best for digging, provide tools, and will cut and clean the best rocks you find for a small fee. After a visit to the ranch you may feel more adventurous and want to go search on your own. The visitor's center has a map of the designated rockhounding areas near Bend. Our favorite is Glass Butte, where you can find all types of really cool, volcanic, glass-like obsidian.

Richard's Rock Ranch, 6683 NE Haycreek Rd., Madras, OR
(541) 475-2680, richardsonrockranch.com

MAKE A SPLASH
AT SHARC

Summertime has arrived! The high desert heat is blazing, school's out, no more snow, and literally every kid in Central Oregon is excited and asking to go to Sunriver Homeowners Aquatic & Recreation Center (SHARC). Be a good parent and don't let your child miss out. The indoor facility is open year-round and other seasons are less crowded, but the waterslides and the jungle gym in the outdoor pool are what kids love most. Better yet, climb a rock wall, play a game of disc golf, or shoot some hoops first to get a workout, all onsite at SHARC. The Lazy River will feel so much more refreshing afterwards.

57250 Overlook Rd., Sunriver, OR
(541) 585-5000, sunriversharc.com

SLED LIKE CHEVY CHASE
AT WANOGA SNO-PARK

If you recognize the title reference from the movie *Christmas Vacation*, be prepared to experience the sled ride of your life! At Wanoga Snow Play Area Sno-Park there is a huge, steep hill right near the parking lot that screams, "Slide down me!" It's really not difficult to climb and you can go up as far as you like: the farther, the faster. Then, yell with nervous glee as you sled uncontrollably down the hill at a hundred miles an hour. (Not really, but it feels fast and it's better than a ride at the amusement park.) But be careful! On crowded days, not everyone has sense enough to get out of the way, and it is difficult to stop once you get started. Smaller hills are strewn around the park as well for younger kids and those who might want to practice first before going all out.

Cascades Lakes Highway
(541) 383-5300, fs.usda.gov/recarea/deschutes/recarea/?recid=38542

TIP

Sleds can be purchased at several hardware stores or retailers around Bend, and in fact, you may want to get one off season. We tried three stores before we found ours because the others were sold out! Spend a few extra bucks and purchase a quality sled. Otherwise, you may end up breaking the cheap plastic one on your second slide like I did.

TURN INTO AN ICICLE
AT TAMOLITCH BLUE POOL

It's a sweltering day. A fun but exhausting hike through the forest along the McKenzie River has you sweating. But then, after a few miles on the trail, you arrive at the destination and are overwhelmed by the beautiful turquoise color of the water. You have arrived at the Tamolitch Pool, one of the most stunning wonders of Central Oregon. Even at a chilly 37 degrees, the pool is definitely worth a swim, or at least a quick dip. Few people last long or get more than their feet wet. Still, the views of the rushing falls and the contrasting reflection of surrounding alders and evergreens on the water make you want to stick around and relish nature at its finest. The color of the water will linger in your mind long after the trip.

National Forest Rd. 2672–655, McKenzie Bridge, OR
(541) 822-3381, fs.usda.gov/recarea/willamette/recarea/?recid=82063

TIP

Careful! About the time the pool becomes visible you will be overlooking it from atop a 70-foot-or-so ledge and may be tempted to jump. Even though the water can be up to 30 feet deep in some places, jumping from the cliff can be dangerous and people often get hurt, either from the jump or from the surprise of the frigid water!

HEAR THE MIGHTY ROAR
OF STEELHEAD FALLS

Tumalo Falls (#63) is the highest waterfall near Bend, but Steelhead Falls might be the most scenic. A short, half-mile hike takes you to the falls where there is plenty of space to picnic, fish, or just sit, watch, and listen to the powerful falls roaring over the boulders. You can stop there and be satisfied with the natural beauty of the world, but I suggest hiking the four-mile loop that steadily climbs up to the ridge and offers views of the Cascade peaks. Surrounded by cliffs millions of years old, you get a sense of appreciation for the world and feel lucky to be part of it. Take a rest and breathe in the crisp, fresh air. On the return route, you will probably want to stop at the falls once more to take in their beauty before returning to civilization. Take your time, relax, and plan another hike like this in the near future.

SW River Rd., Terrebonne, OR
(541) 416-6700, blm.gov/visit/steelhead-falls-trail

PREPARE TO BE AWESTRUCK
AT CRATER LAKE NATIONAL PARK

If you are anywhere near Bend, Crater Lake National Park should be included on your itinerary. About a two-hour drive away, this amazing destination is one of the most beautiful spots in the United States. Formed thousands of years ago from climactic volcanic eruptions, the deepest lake in the United States has a mesmerizing 'crater blue' color that you will never see anywhere else. Take the Rim Drive around the caldera that allows multiple scenic viewpoints of the lake. Explore farther by walking the numerous short trails leading to even more astounding views. If you really want to witness the best the area has to offer, camp for a night or two and hike the longer trails. However you choose to visit Oregon's only national park, this destination should be a priority on your bucketlist.

Crater Lake, OR
(541) 594-3000, nps.gov/crla/index.htm

FISH
THE PLENTIFUL WATERS
OF CENTRAL OREGON

Whether you want to relax on the bank of a stream or battle the toughest of fish species, Bend and the surrounding area is a true fisherman's paradise. The rivers, streams, lakes, and ponds are plentiful and pristine. Trout are the most popular quarry, but you can also catch bass, steelhead, and other prized species when you cast your line. Younger and novice fishermen may want to begin at Shevlin Pond or Pine Nursery Pond. Many seasoned anglers fish the Crooked River for its scenery and the Metolius River for the challenge. Fly fishing is the most exciting style to learn, and once you know how to land a fly accurately you will be hooked, but luckily not like the fish!

Shevlin Pond in Shevlin Park, 18920 NW Shevlin Park Rd.

Pine Nursery Pond in Bend Pine Park, 3750 NE Purcell Blvd.

TIP

Be sure to check the regulations
(permits, limits, etc.) before setting out to fish.
Not only is this the right thing to do
to preserve the aquatic life, but it might
also save you from paying a fine later!

TAKE
THE PAULINA PLUNGE

What is the Paulina Plunge, you ask? Well, it's a full day of exciting fun on the Newberry National Volcanic Monument, but first let me set up the scene: A tour bus shuttles spirited groups of participants into the Oregon backcountry while the guide shares stories about the local indigenous people and the saga of Chief Paulina. Once you arrive in the midst of the scenic Paulina Mountains, you get a fat-tire bike for the downhill journey, which means it's time to descend about 2000 feet, bringing you back close to where you started. Even more thrilling are the stops along the way. Several waterfalls break up the ride so you can park the bikes, soak up the views, and take a dip in the cool water. Two of the falls form natural waterslides where most of the group will be sliding or jumping from boulders into the pristine pools. It's the perfect mix of physical activity and laid-back fun.

53750 US-97, La Pine, OR
(541) 389-0562, paulinaplunge.com

GET YOUR SURF ON
AT BEND WHITEWATER PARK

The closest ocean to Bend is about a three-hour drive, but this doesn't stop surf enthusiasts from catching some serious waves. At Bend Whitewater Park the Deschutes River has been transformed into three passageways; a habitat channel to protect river health and wildlife, a passageway channel for those who are floating the river (#56), and a whitewater channel that allows seasoned surfers and kayakers to practice their craft. Onlookers can watch with awe from Columbia Street Bridge or McKay Park. Those with enough audacity and experience can get out on the whitewater channel and join the fun. Even on the coldest days of winter you may see hardcore surfers in their wetsuits trying to catch that perfect wave!

166 SW Shevlin Hixon Dr.
(541) 389-7275, bendparksandrec.org/facility/bend-whitewater-park

FLOAT OR PADDLEBOARD
THE DESCHUTES RIVER

Cutting through the center of Bend, the Deschutes River remains nearly pristine and seems like the lifeline of the city. The stretch between Farewell Bend Park and Mirror Pond is one of the most popular spots to float, especially on a hot sweltering day. Not too fast, not too slow, the river flows at the perfect speed to allow for a gentle, laid-back experience as you pass through the Old Mill, soak up the sun, and marvel at the surrounding Cascades. Purchase an innertube, an air mattress, or paddleboard (basically anything that floats) if you plan to get on the river often. Chances are strong that the trip will become a summer ritual. You can also rent from outfitters like Tumalo Creek Kayak & Canoe or Sun Country Tours. Once you disembark at Drake Park you can catch a shuttle that returns to River Bend Park, the most popular launch area, where you can start all over again

Tumalo Creek Kayak & Canoe, 805 SW Industrial Way
(541) 317-9407, tumalocreek.com/river-tube-rental

Sun Country Tours, 531 SW 13th St.
(541) 382-1709, suncountrytours.com

BUILD THOSE LEG MUSCLES
AT PHIL'S TRAILHEAD

When I was a kid I dreamed of competing in the X Games. Life happened, and there were hardly any good biking trails where I lived, so the dream faded. Then, when I moved to Bend and discovered Phil's Trailhead, the fire was rekindled. According to many local mountain bikers, Phil's has the reputation for the best biking around Bend. With roughly 60 miles of trails, the area doesn't ever seem crowded, and all skill levels are represented. Veteran riders can endure the brutal uphill climbs, roots, rocks and other obstacles. I plan to slowly work my way up to those more exhilarating technical rides like the COD but for now, I'll stick to the mostly flat-but-fun Phil's-Ben's Loop. Keep an eye out for my name at the 2025 X Games.

bendtrails.org/trail/phils-trail-complex

DRIVE
THE PICTURESQUE
CASCADE LAKES SCENIC BYWAY

It would take more than a lifetime to fully explore the area surrounding Bend, but a perfect place to start is the Cascade Lakes Scenic Byway. You will be awed by just a day trip driving the scenic road through the mountains without ever leaving the car. Better yet, stop at a few of the fourteen alpine lakes, get your feet wet, or snap some photos of the Cascade Mountains reflected in the crystal clear waters. Maybe watch a sunset or have a picnic. You can also view at least sixteen interpretive sites along the highway that were selected for conservation education, gorgeous views, and/or access to the Deschutes River and Cascade Lakes. Chances are you will feel the urge to return and dive deeper into this majestic area.

Cascades Lake Scenic Byway
traveloregon.com/things-to-do/trip-ideas/scenic-drives/
cascades-lakes-scenic-byway

TIP

To submerge yourself in the miracle of this area, you should visit one lake at a time and spend the day (or more) there. Every lake has distinctive features, whether it's Hosmer Lake for fishing, Elk Lake for swimming, or Sparks Lake for peaceful kayaking. Most locals have a favorite. And although the lakes are most popular during the summer, the change of seasons brings a change of scenery worth checking out all year long.

TAKE YOURSELF OUT TO THE BALLGAME
WITH THE BEND ELKS

Bend may not have a professional sports team, but that doesn't stop fans from avidly supporting local amateur baseball. The Bend Elks play June through August at Vince Genna Stadium so during the summer months it's all about the hot dogs, peanuts, and sodas while you spend the afternoon watching America's favorite pastime. Baseball has a long history in Bend, and a number of teams have played in town for decades. That said, here's a quick fun fact: Kurt Russell, the actor, once played for the Bend Rainbows, one of the previous Bend baseball teams. Today's Elks have been playing in the West Coast Baseball League since 2000. After participating in all the outdoor activities around here, it's nice to sit back and be a spectator.

Vince Genna Stadium, 401 SE Roosevelt Ave.
(541) 312-9259, bendelks.com

STAY ACTIVE DURING WINTER
AT THE PAVILION

Bendites love their winter sports, and you can bet if it's not cold or snowy enough to play outside, they will go to the Pavilion to satisfy their urges. This state-of-the-art facility has a huge NHL-size sheet of ice, perfect for sliding and gliding. But that's not all. Ever tried curling? Me neither, but after seeing how much fun folks were having while playing, I plan to try it. Take ice skating classes, join a curling league, play on a hockey team, or just drop by for an open skate. Even as a spectator, you can keep warm in the viewing room or at a fire pit outside. And don't think the Pavilion sits idle during the summer. They offer sports camps and classes galore!

1001 SW Bradbury Dr.
(541) 389-7588, bendparksandrec.org/facility/the-pavilion

STROLL THROUGH
DRAKE PARK

How about an idyllic stroll along the scenic Mirror Pond? Up for a quiet picnic where you can just let the kids or the dog run around and play? Keep meaning to schedule a meet-up for a bike ride with friends? You can do all this and more at Drake Park. The acres of open lawn, striking views of the water, and proximity to downtown make this park a favorite in Bend. During spring and summer all sorts of festivals and events take place, like Munch & Music (#31) and the 4th of July Celebration after the Pet Parade (#39). If you are lucky, you may spot one of the great horned owls that make the park their home. If not, you will most definitely see a Canadian goose or a thousand.

777 NW Riverside Blvd.
bendparksandrec.org/park/drake-park-and-mirror-pond

SIGN UP
FOR A HIKE OR WALK
WITH THE DESCHUTES LAND TRUST

There is so much to know about nature, and the more I play outside, the stronger my thirst to learn becomes. The Deschutes Land Trust holds informative events throughout the year to educate those of us interested in the outdoors. The trust is a nonprofit organization with a mission to conserve and protect lands in Central Oregon. It is run primarily on donations and with the help of volunteers. My favorite events are the numerous walks and hikes that begin in Spring. Each is geared towards a particular topic like bird or wildflower identification or geology, and there is even a hike that gives tips about nature journaling. Others, like the butterfly walk, are ideal for kids. I may never know everything there is to know about the Central Oregon wilderness, but every time I explore the nature preserves with outdoor experts, I come away feeling a bit more knowledgeable.

210 NW Irving Ave., Ste. 102
(541) 330-0017, deschuteslandtrust.org

VIEW THE CASCADES
OF TUMALO FALLS

The tallest, most photogenic waterfall in Central Oregon is right in Bend's backyard. Tumalo Falls roars over a cliff nearly 100 feet high. Imagine that power slowly wearing large boulders down to pebbles over millions of years. For instant gratification, snap your photos of the falls at the scenic overlook where most people stop. It roars over the cliff, literally a few feet from the parking lot. To explore the natural beauty in more depth, follow the trail upward to countless other smaller cascades and get a grand view from the top of Tumalo Falls. Still farther in, you can follow the creek along the trail and suddenly be engulfed in a forest of fir, hemlock, manzanita, and other native vegetation. If you like to camp, Happy Valley awaits, or you can make a loop and return to the parking lot. In my opinion, the greater rewards are those buried deeper in the forest.

fs.usda.gov/recarea/deschutes/recarea/?recid=38526

TRAIL RUN
THROUGH ARCHIE BRIGGS CANYON

Miles and miles of amazing trails. Which is the best for running? The goal is to try them all eventually, but my favorite is the Archie Briggs Canyon Trail. Part of the Deschutes River Trail (#46), you will forget about distance and complexity and instead let the spectacular surroundings guide your way. Gaze down at the roaring river from high cliffs. Dash through manzanita, rabbitbrush, and sagebrush. During summer the wildflowers will brighten your run with colors. Depending on how far you want to go (the farther the better), you can start or stop at several points. A favorite entry point of mine is Sawyer Park. A good nature run is not only good for your physical health but for your mental and spiritual health as well. What are you waiting for? Get outside!

hikespeak.com/trails/archie-briggs-canyon-hike-bend-oregon

FEED THE CUTE ALPACAS
AT CRESCENT MOON RANCH

Driving along Highway 97 you stare out of the window and suddenly notice a bunch of cute, furry creatures in the fields. "Were those alpacas?" your child asks as the family does a double take. Alpacas are not something you see every day, but if you drive by Crescent Moon Ranch, there they are, waiting for a visit. Stop by and interact with them during visiting hours: winter 10 a.m.–4 p.m.; summer 9 a.m.–5 p.m., seven days a week. You can purchase grain and feed them, all the while taking in the picturesque views of Smith Rock (#63) and the Cascade Mountains in the background. An onsite boutique sells items made from the highly sought-after alpaca fiber, known to produce some of the most luxurious textile products in the world. After getting to know some of their distinct personalities, you may even want to take an alpaca home. And guess what? You can! Just ask the owners for details before loading one up in the car.

7566 N Hwy 97, Terrebonne, OR
(541) 923-2285, crescentmoonranch.com

HIKE MISERY TRAIL
AND LIVE TO TELL ABOUT IT

Central Oregon is full of natural wonders and picturesque landscapes. Smith Rock State Park in Terrebonne is no exception. Although you will never catch me scaling the massive rhyolite rock formations, the park is considered a paradise among the rock-climbing community. For those of us content to enjoy the scenery with two feet on the ground, hiking is a fulfilling alternative. Misery Trail, the most popular route, meanders through deep canyons and climbs up and down steep ridges to give awesome views of the Crooked River and the Cascade snowpeaks. The hike is not easy, but the incomparable views make every step worth the effort. Bring binoculars to spot golden eagles as they soar high above you, magpies hiding in the brush, or other animals following their daily routines. Most likely you will glimpse climbers on the cliffs along the route and stare up at them in awe, especially if they are dangling from the towering Monkey Face Rock, the park's most iconic feature. Someday you may be one of those brave souls!

Smith Rock State Park, Terrebonne, OR
(541) 516-0054, smithrock.com

TIP

On any trail, always take plenty of water, a snack, and sunscreen. And please follow basic hiking etiquette, the rules of which are usually posted in several places in the park: Stay on the trails. Keep dogs on a leash. Pack out what you packed in. These rules are in place for a reason—to keep these scenic areas protected and beautiful. Don't be those guys (or girls) who say to themselves, "Well, if I do it, it's OK." If everyone thought that way, these areas would lose a lot of what makes them so special.

EXPLORE UNDERGROUND
INSIDE THE LAVA RIVER CAVE

Imagine a river of molten lava from an erupting volcano flowing underground and carving a tunnel. This is what happened centuries ago, and nowadays, you can actually walk through the same spot. At the Newberry National Monument (#67), you can descend into the darkness of the Lava River Cave for a self-guided tour and witness what the dynamic forces of nature have created over thousands of years. You'll be fascinated by lavacicles, gardens of spires and pinnacles in the sand, and other cave features. You can even eavesdrop on a stranger's conversation from across the cave due to the peculiar arched construction of Echo Hall. If you really fancy yourself a spelunker (one who studies caves), you can explore the last few hundred feet of the cave on your hands and knees. The cave is open from May through September.

Newberry National Monument
fs.usda.gov/recarea/deschutes/recarea/?recid=38396

TIP

There is no charge to enter the cave but there is a $5 parking fee for a day pass, unless you have a recreation pass. Flashlights can also be rented, and the site recommends bringing TWO light sources. Also of note: close-toed shoes are recommended AND visitors are asked not to wear clothes they have worn in other caves to prevent the spread of White-nose Syndrome, which has wiped out large numbers of bats. And be sure to bring a jacket. It gets chilly down there!

PRETEND TO BE ON ANOTHER PLANET
AT NEWBERRY NATIONAL MONUMENT

About 1,300 years ago the Newberry Volcano erupted in Central Oregon. Though still a hotspot (pun intended) of volcanic activity, the threat of a possible eruption doesn't stop people from moving here in droves. At Newberry National Monument you can see why they come when you witness the results of the thousands of years' worth of geologic upheaval that created this magnificent landscape. As you walk trails like the Big Obsidian Flow you'll notice jagged obsidian gleaming brightly in the sun. These shiny black rocks, combined with the pumice and lack of vegetation, make you feel as if you are walking on another planet. From the Paulina Peak Trail, you get a panorama of Central Oregon and the Newberry Caldera. There are so many trails to explore and each provides its own particular version of these otherworldly geologic features. Stop by the Lava Lands Visitor Center to get more information.

(541) 383-5300, fs.usda.gov/recarea/deschutes/recarea/?recid=66159

HEAR THE ROAR OF THE MIGHTY RAPIDS
AT BENHAM AND DILLON FALLS

All this talk about waterfalls, turquoise blue waters, snowcapped peaks, and other natural phenomena has probably got you thinking Central Oregon is the stuff of dreams. It is, and let me add another worthwhile hike to prove my point. The trek from Benham Falls to Dillon Falls showcases some of the most spectacular views of the Deschutes River: towering ponderosas, fields of otherworldly lava rock, wildflowers (in summer), and other native vegetation year-round. All the while the river roars beside you. In fact, the falls are not really waterfalls, but the largest set of rapids on the Deschutes. If you've hiked the entirety of the Deschutes River Trail (#45) you will have passed these points, but since they are a ways out of town, most people drive to them, park, get a glimpse, and return to Bend. Don't just get a taste; walk the trail to get the full meal.

fs.usda.gov/recarea/deschutes/recarea/?recid=38340
fs.usda.gov/recarea/deschutes/recarea/?recid=38288

STEP
ON A CRACK IN THE GROUND

You might ask, "What's so great about a crack in the ground? I can look down at the sidewalk to see one of those." Well, you can hike at the bottom of this one. Around 70 feet deep, two miles long, and only wide enough for one person in some places, the crack is really a large volcanic fissure. Since the climate of Christmas Valley is so dry, it has never been filled up with soil and rock, meaning it hasn't changed much in thousands of years, but there has been rockfall in places so getting through requires a bit of scrambling. But as dry as the area is, you will be pleasantly surprised. On scorching hot days, a hike through the Crack can actually be refreshing. The temperature is 20 degrees cooler at the bottom than it was at the rim. Bright green moss stretches up the cliffs where birds fly to and from their nests. If you want a quiet hike, free from the crowds, you've come to the right place.

Christmas Valley, OR
blm.gov/visit/crack-in-the-ground

GET FIT OR TAKE A DIP
AT JUNIPER SWIM & FITNESS

In a city where outdoor sports reign supreme, health is a top priority. Run by Bend Parks and Recreation (#69), Juniper Swim & Fitness Center is my 'go to' place when I can't get outside. More than an average gym, the clean facilities, modern equipment, outdoor and indoor pools, saunas, and much more create the perfect environment for health and wellness. Juniper has countless family activities and classes available, ranging from yoga to cycling to swimming and more. Not a member? No worries, they have flexible options to meet your needs. Purchase a punch card that allows several visits with access to all the amenities. Drop-ins are welcome as well. If you want to stay fit and healthy and be part of a tight-knit community, this is your place.

800 NE 6th St.
(541) 389-7665, bendparksandrec.org/fitness-swim/juniper-swim-fitness

REACH NEW HEIGHTS
AT BEND ROCK GYM

For those not quite ready to climb real rock formations like those at Smith Rock State Park (#65), the Bend Rock Gym still promises a sense of adventure. It also offers serious climbers the chance to hone their skills when they might not have time to get to the real rocks. Three types of admission allow you to climb on your own schedule: day passes, punch cards, and monthly memberships. Bring your own or rent gear and climb until you are sore. Oh yeah, you will feel it the next day. All levels are welcome, even young children. The gym provides harnesses and other safety equipment and makes sure you know how to use it before you ascend the walls. Most employees are experienced climbers who can guide and give safety tips. Talk about a great way to test your toughness and develop a skill! The higher you go the higher your adrenaline and confidence get.

1182 SE Centennial Ct.
(541) 388-6764, bendrockgym.com

STAND ON TOP OF A VOLCANO
AT PILOT BUTTE STATE PARK

Yes, you read the intro correctly. Bend is one of the few cities in the Unites States to have a volcano located within the city limits. No worries though, Pilot Butte isn't erupting anytime soon—at least we hope not! For the best experience start an hour or so before sunset and hike one of the mile-long trails to the summit. Along the trails, the strong scents of Juniper trees and other high-desert brush quickly make you forget you are still in the city. If you prefer an easier route, drive the scenic road that lazily spirals around the cone. On top, breathe the crisp air and peer out at the amazing 360-degree view that includes the entire city, the high desert, and the magnificent Cascade Mountains. Then try to fathom the fact that you are standing on top of a volcano!

(541) 388-6055, oregonstateparks.org/index.cfm?do=parkPage.dsp_
parkPage&parkId=33

BREATHE IN
THE SWEET SMELLS
OF TUMALO LAVENDER

At Tumalo Lavender the breeze carries a delightful aroma through the air and immediately you feel relaxed and calm. Shades of purple stretch across the ten-acre farm and represent the many varieties of lavender in meticulously planted rows. The plant grows exceptionally well in the Pacific Northwest and this place proves it. Walk through the fields and admire the countless butterflies and bees purposefully pollinating the plants. Gordon and Judy Knight, the owners, will happily explain anything you want to know about lavender and show you the process by which they make the oil. Meanwhile, their friendly dog chills out lazily in the fields. After a while at this laid-back farm, you may want to take a nap yourself.

19825 Connarn Rd.
(541) 383-2441, tumalolavender.com

HELP GROW A GARDEN
AT THE ENVIRONMENTAL CENTER

Calling all volunteers! During the summer months children (and adults) are invited to help grow a garden at the Environmental Center. In this outdoor classroom, folks get their hands dirty by planting tomatoes, peppers, and other veggies, and caring for them during growing season. One minute the children might be digging or making observations and the next minute they might be chasing other kids around the garden. What better way to learn about where our food comes from? The adults often help, and for their efforts the would-be farmers are generously furnished with hydrating beverages (including beer—for adults only). Hey, working in the garden (especially with kids) deserves a drink!

The Environmental Center also offers lots of other year-round community activities and educational events. Be sure to check those out as well.

16 NW Kansas Ave.
(541) 385-6908, envirocenter.org

DEFY DEATH
BUNGEE JUMPING OVER
THE CROOKED RIVER

For the adrenaline junkies reading this book, this excerpt tops the list. Many sightseers visit Peter Skene Ogden State Park and the Crooked River High Bridge to take in the spectacular panoramic views of the gorge and surrounding Cascades. Others feel the need to get their blood pumping. Central Oregon Bungee Adventures will satisfy the bravest of thrill seekers. James Scott, the owner, has years of experience and offers jumps during the summer months. From atop the bridge, daring souls dive 250 feet, the longest of any commercial bungee jump in the United States! It's an insane way to enjoy the surroundings and one you are sure never to forget. Talk about a rush! Is once not enough? Subsequent jumps are cheaper. Be sure get videos of the experience so the grandkids will believe you one day.

Central Oregon Bungee Adventures
Crooked River High Bridge, 12797 Hwy 97
(541) 668-5867, oregonbungee.com

CULTURE AND HISTORY

BECOME AN ART CRITIC
ON THE FIRST FRIDAY ART WALK

Every first Friday of the month lively crowds descend on the streets of downtown and the Old Mill District to enjoy the First Friday Art Walk. The event has become a popular tradition in Bend, and yes, throughout the day you will see paintings and sculptures and such, but during the night you will also be able to appreciate many other types of artists displaying their skills. Think about the chef, the musician, the clothing designer, the vintner, the photographer, the jewelry maker; all are masters of their respective crafts. Dozens of businesses stay open late, many offering live music and free snacks and drinks. The night is an amazing opportunity to mingle with friends, meet new people, and celebrate the city's eclectic and diverse art scene.

Downtown & Old Mill District
facebook.com/FirstFridayBend

SOAK UP THE HISTORY
OF CENTRAL OREGON

Once upon a time the Deschutes Historical Museum housed rowdy yet studious schoolchildren in what was the first 'modern school' built in Bend. Nowadays, it houses an in-depth view into the history of Central Oregon. Browse the building to get educated about this fascinating region of the country. *Ms. Reid's Classroom* travels back in time to what a classroom looked like over 100 years ago. My kids wanted to spend most of the visit playing teacher and student in this room. Logging, which has had a tremendous influence on Oregon's past, is detailed in the *Forests of Central Oregon* exhibit. Still other rooms have artifacts and information about Native Americans, the pioneer days, and the earliest days of Bend. If you have questions after visiting the rooms, be sure to ask the staff. Each is an encyclopedia of information when it comes to the deep history of the area.

129 NW Idaho Ave.
(541) 389-1813, deschuteshistory.org

EXPLORE THE CLIMATE OF CENTRAL OREGON
AT THE HIGH DESERT MUSEUM

Oregon gets a bad rap for being wet and dreary much of the year, but that is not so in this part of the state. The high desert enjoys mostly sunshine during the year. At the High Desert Museum, the story of Central Oregon's climate is told through art, Native American history, science, wildlife, and more. All these mediums create a textured and interactive learning experience that make both kids and adults want to return again and again. With nine to twelve rotating exhibits, you can never see it all because the museum constantly changes and provides new, innovative ways to educate the public. Permanent exhibits like the *Spirit of the West* display the history of the Paiute people and other past residents of Central Oregon. Residents like the otters and the porcupines are local favorites. My family is partial to the mighty raptors at the Birds of Prey Center. There is nothing quite like witnessing the power of a bald eagle by seeing it up close and looking directly into its fearless gaze.

59800 US-97
(541) 382-4754, highdesertmuseum.org

LOITER IN THE ALLEYS
OF DOWNTOWN

The Tin Pan Alley Art Collection livens up the alleys and even the parking garages of downtown Bend. With more than a dozen pieces and counting, the city has transformed these usually dingy, smelly areas to culturally significant attractions. Blink an eye and you might not find it, but Tin Pan Alley itself is absolutely worth a stop. Take a self-guided tour to view paintings like *The Visitor* hanging along the brick walls. During the morning, duck into Lone Pine Coffee Roasters for a beverage. If you are there in the evening, catch an independent film at Tin Pan Theater, an almost hidden microcinema with an intimate retro vibe. Never have you seen city alleyways so inviting! An extension of this brand of public art can be found in the Old Mill District (#83, 90) as well.

Tin Pan Alley Art Collection
visitbend.com/things-to-do/art-museums-history/arts/tin-pan-alley-art

Lone Pine Coffee Roasters, 910 NW Harriman St.
(541) 306-1010

Tin Pan Theater, 869 NW Tin Pan Alley
(541) 241-2271

ADMIRE UNIQUE ART
WHILE DRIVING THE ROUNDABOUTS

When driving in Bend, you may get the feeling you are in Europe with all the roundabouts. They take some getting used to, but you will quickly notice that many roundabouts in Bend have stunning works of art in the middle. In fact, soon you will be driving out of your way to make sure you find *Phoenix Rising*, *Sound Garden* (not the band), and *Sunrise Spirit Column* (a few of my favorites). I would not advise stopping in busy traffic to take a pic or to admire the art, but there are usually places to park nearby. Bend has over twenty sculptures in total and searching for them all is a great way to get to know the city. *Yakaya* is my overall favorite, a large flower-like sculpture located in River Bend Park and made from full-size, colorful kayaks. Pretty impressive!

All around town
artinpublicplaces.org/roundabout.html

TIP

Visit Bend has a Roundabout Art Route brochure with a map and detailed information about each of the art installations. And, like the Bend Ale Trail, you can visit several of them, return to the visitor's center, and claim a prize! Be sure to pay attention to what you see though, because they quiz you on this one!

SPEND A DAY (OR MORE)
IN SISTERS

Most states tend to have that one little place full of culture and vibrant energy, an area that seems to draw artists to it. In Oregon, the town is Sisters, located about half an hour from Bend. With the glorious mountain backdrop, the town could itself be a painting. Start by grabbing a coffee from Sisters Coffee so you have something to sip as you take a leisurely walk along the lively streets. Visit as many galleries and shops as possible along the way (too many to name here) and view the public art as well. You will be amazed by the talent and variety of what you see. Chances are, you will be inspired to create your own art or at least leave Sisters with new items to decorate your home.

Sisters
sistersoregonguide.com

Sisters Coffee, 273 W Hood Ave., Sisters, OR 97759
(541) 549-0527, sisterscoffee.com

FEEL THE PULSE OF BEND
IN THE OLD MILL DISTRICT

Before becoming the booming tourist town it is today, Bend was home to two of the largest lumber mills in the country. World War I produced a large demand for timber, and by the end of World War II, the beautiful forests of the West were nearly decimated. Fast forward to the present: Standing in the middle of the Old Mill District you are in an outdoor, modern-day shopping mall (#90), but this spot is exactly where the mills were located, and the rivers were jammed with logs. Walk along the trail adjacent to the Deschutes River and among the shops and restaurants to read the interpretive signs about Bend's past as a mill town. To see the pictures of what the area used to look like compared to the present is really phenomenal, proof that we can sustain and even regenerate our planet. The most obvious tributes to the city's past are the large iconic smokestacks towering above the REI building which can be seen from almost anywhere in Bend. Elsewhere, the concrete foundation for a mill powerhouse remains intact and has become a colorful box garden for flowers in spring. Modern murals, paintings (part of the Tin Pan Alley Art Collection), and sculptures are also strewn throughout the district, creating the perfect mixture of Bend's proud past and present. The city is working hard to ensure its future as well.

450 SW Powerhouse Dr., Ste. 422
(541) 312-0131, oldmilldistrict.com

WALK
THE HISTORIC SITES OF BEND

Incorporated in 1904, Bend is relatively young, but it still has a deep history. Like many cities around the world, it is built up around a river. If you feel like getting educated about the Central Oregon past, pick up a free Bend Historic Sites map at the Deschutes Historical Museum (#78) where the museum is also No. 1 on the list. From there, all 45 locations on the map are located within walking distance. You can take a leisurely stroll and visit places like Alexander Drake's homesite (the founder of Bend) and the J.J. West Building (the town's first stone structure). Some locations have plaques with more detailed information. The walk is definitely doable in a day, but you can also break it up and take as long as you like. By the time you finish you will be a Bend history expert!

Bend Historic Sites, all around town

Deschutes Historical Museum, 129 NW Idaho Ave.
(541) 389-1813, deschuteshistory.org

PONDER THE COSMOS
WHILE YOU DRINK A BREW

Space, the final frontier. Picture this scenario: You're philosophizing with friends over drinks about our place in the vast universe. The sky is clear with a new moon and the stars are shining brightly. You decide to get up from the patio and walk upstairs to the Hopservatory to view the cosmos more closely. This fantasy can become reality at Worthy Brewing (yes, the brewery in # 7). Begin your tour of the Hopservatory downstairs in the Transporter Room where the entire area is decorated with colorful mosaic tiles that illustrate the universe. TV monitors provide the latest cosmic information. Walk upstairs to the Dome and see a stunning panorama ranging from Mount Hood to Mount Bachelor (#43). On Thursday through Sunday evenings and sometimes during special 'lunar' events, Grant, the Hopservatory's resident astronomer, will show you the brightest objects in the sky through the powerful telescope. Combining astronomy and a night out with friends has never been so fun!

495 NE Bellevue Dr.
(541) 639-4776, worthygardenclub.com/hopservatory.html

SURROUND YOURSELF WITH TALENT
AT ART IN THE HIGH DESERT

If I could choose one talent to acquire, I would want to be an artist. Then I could be one of the hundreds of artists from around the country who vie for a coveted spot in the Art in the High Desert Craft Show & Fair. If I were really lucky, I would be one of the 120 who make the cut. But until then, I'll have to be content attending the Bend event, one of the top ten art shows in the Unites States. For three days in August, phenomenal art of all types is displayed and sold on the banks of the Deschutes River. Paintings, ceramics, photos, jewelry, glass, crafted wood furniture and carvings, and more; at least fifteen categories are represented. It's impossible to leave without new décor for the house and a desire to go home and be creative.

The Banks of the Deschutes River in the Old Mill District
(541) 322-6272, artinthehighdesert.com

VIEW GALAXIES FAR FAR AWAY
AT PINE MOUNTAIN OBSERVATORY

Billions and billions of stars in the sky and because of bright city lights we rarely see them. Not so in this part of Oregon. In the less populated parts of Bend and especially outside of the city the stars are fascinating even with the naked eye. But to really be "starstruck" a visit to the Pine Mountain Observatory is mandatory. The mixture of elevation, clean air, and pitch- dark surroundings allow for perfect stargazing conditions. Although the observatory is used mostly for research, on weekends from Memorial Day until the end of September anyone can visit and get intimate with the cosmos. Astronomers on hand will point out the visible features of the night sky to novice viewers. After spending a clear evening communing with the night sky, you will leave with a new perspective on our place in the universe.

56100 Pine Mountain Rd.
(541) 382-8331, pmo.uoregon.edu

RAISE YOUR AWARENESS
AT SUNRIVER NATURE CENTER

Sometimes even wild creatures like ospreys, eagles, and beavers need a little tender loving care. Often they are sick or hurt and need to be rescued. Fortunately, places like Sunriver Nature Center exist as a sanctuary for injured or native birds and small mammals. And during the time that the Center attempts to rehabilitate them, we get to learn. For a small admission fee you can listen to experts teach all about the birds of prey and other native species. Visitors can even get up close and personal with amphibians or snakes. Strolls through the botanical garden and around the Aspen Lake Loop provide glimpses of native plants and maybe an occasional otter. The onsite Oregon Observatory provides views of the skies. When you find yourself wanting to know more about local wildlife, or maybe to make friends with a resident raptor, the center is a perfect day trip.

57245 River Rd., Sunriver, OR
(541) 593-4394, sunrivernaturecenter.org

BECOME MESMERIZED
BY THE ART OF ALFRED A. DOLEZAL

Visionary artist Alfred A. Dolezal is originally from Austria but he has lived in Central Oregon for many years. A trip to his gallery in Redmond is one you will always remember. In his paintings the vivid colors seem to jump out of the canvas. The profound symbolism may take a lifetime to uncover and causes observers to explore their own deep thoughts and feelings. Works such as *Triumph Over Adversity* and *The Harmony of Opposites* are based on timeless parables. *Light Through the Ages* depicts the many people who have influenced not only Dolezal's work, but all human progress. Behind every painting is an intricate story. If you are lucky, the artist himself may be at the gallery to explain his thought process while he created each work. Prepare to question your own beliefs and become mesmerized by some amazingly complex art.

7525 Falcon Crest Dr., Ste. 100, Redmond, OR
(541) 526-1185, alfreddolezal.com

SHOPPING AND FASHION

SHOP 'TIL YOU DROP
IN THE OLD MILL DISTRICT

Bend's biggest shopping area, the Old Mill District, is located in the heart of the city (#83). With over forty stores, several restaurants, and a movie theatre, this open-air mall is nestled on the Deschutes River. You will find many of the well-known anchor stores like Victoria's Secret, Claire's, REI, Banana Republic, and other favorites along with one-of-a-kind boutique shops. Restaurants for all tastes are strategically placed throughout the mall. It's not a bad place to just hang out either. For those who have finished their shopping, there are opportunities to take a walk on the bridge or traverse the paved trails to enjoy beautiful views of the river and mountains while you wait for the other shoppers in your group. You can even bring your running shoes and get some exercise while everyone else in your party spends money.

450 SW Powerhouse Dr., Ste. 422
(541) 312-0131, oldmilldistrict.com

SIP A BEER
WHILE YOU SHOP
AT REVOLVR MENSWEAR

"Would you like to try a Porter from Cascade Lake Brewery?" I looked around, unsure if the retail clerk at REVOLVR Menswear was talking to me. "Uh, sure." A minute later I had a half pint of a refreshing beer in my hand. This had to be best strategy ever to keep a customer inside the store longer or was it a onetime thing? Nope, it happens without fail, every visit, and usually a different type of beer is offered each time. But even without the free beverage, REVOLVR has the coolest, most stylish apparel and accessories for men in the city. No matter what season, this should be the first stop when you plan to buy some new threads. No need to rush with the beer and the clerks never press you to buy. Take your time, try on some clothes, or sit and relax in the comfortable leather seats while you decide which rack to browse next.

945 NW Wall St.

(541) 647-2627, revolvrmens.com

STAY FASHIONABLE
AT HOT BOX BETTY

Ladies, I can't leave you out. After all, you are the true fashionistas. Speaking with women around the area, the name of one place popped up more than any other for women's shopping in Bend–Hot Box Betty. Sure enough, this stylish, upscale boutique is on point with all of the hippest clothing and accessories: shoes, apparel, lotions, jewelry, and more. The shop has an impressive variety of merchandise and the Bettys have a penchant for stocking only the highest quality brands. The staff take the time to help you find what suits you best. Check out their social media to get a feel for the vibe. I had to pull my wife out of there! She'll probably return on her own.

903 NW Wall St., Ste. 100
(541) 383-0050, hotboxbetty.com

BUY THE KIDS SOME COOL THREADS
AT HOPSCOTCH KIDS

Those of us with children want them feeling comfortable in their clothes and looking dapper. Last in the clothing department, but definitely not least, Hopscotch Kids carries everything from stylish dress apparel to sporty outdoor gear. You will most likely find what you need here for newborns up through tweens. More than clothing, the store is a one-stop shop. Hopscotch also sells educational and interactive toys, conventional and unconventional board games, puzzles, unique school supplies (often very glittery), jewelry for Mom, and much more. Need ideas for how to decorate a child's room? Once again this is your place. Be prepared: It's one of those shops where your kids may ask a hundred times, "Can I have this?"

1303 NW Galveston Ave.
(541) 213-2245, hopscotch-kids.business.site

SAVOR THE BEST
OF BOTH WORLDS
AT DUDLEY'S BOOKSHOP

There are so many great coffee shops in Bend and there are a quite a few good bookstores as well. Combine the two and you get the best of both worlds at Dudley's Bookstore. Offering both new and used books, Dudley's is a place where you can lounge around for hours and read, order a beverage or pastry, compose on your laptop, study, or read the local news. Downstairs is a little livelier with the café but upstairs you can usually relax more and enjoy the relative quietude and laid-back vibe. And like the coffee shops of old, Dudley's is also where the exchange and flowering of ideas take place; foreign language learners, book clubs, writers' workshops, and other groups meet here on a regular basis. I feel smarter for having been here every time I leave the shop.

135 NW Minnesota
(541) 749-2010, dudleysbookshopcafe.com

PICK UP A SOUVENIR
AT ONE OF THESE SHOPS

Two shops come to mind when I'm buying something with the Bend logo for friends and family (or myself). Yep, the city has its own logo and even its own font. For clothing, especially T-shirts, Cascade Cottons has a large selection of awesome designs, many of which sport the Bend trademark. Nearby and more than a typical souvenir shop, The Bend Store has the items you might expect to find: coffee mugs, stickers, magnets and more. However, as a hub for local artists, the Bend Store also sells handcrafted jewelry, art, and other unique treasures. Don't leave without a quality souvenir to remind you of the good times you had here.

Cascade Cottons, 909 NW Wall St.
(541) 306-6071, cascadecottons.com

The Bend Store, 815 NW Wall St.
(541) 389-4700, bendstore.com

BUILD YOUR VINYL COLLECTION
AT RANCH RECORDS

Vinyl has been making a comeback because it just sounds better and every city (or at least every hip city) should have a record store. Ranch Records boasts Bend's largest collection of vinyl, CDs, concert videos, and even some cassette tapes. But don't think it's all older music; new artists still put their music out on records and CDs. The shop also has the best collection of concert posters I've ever seen from all genres: Snoop Dogg, Widespread Panic, Pearl Jam, The Beatles, and more. Of course, as some of them sell, others take their place. Many of the posters are even autographed. Back in the '90s I used to get super hyped for Tuesdays when new music was released at the local music shop. Nowadays, it's New Music Fridays, but any day I walk into Ranch Records I get excited about music all over again!

117 NW Oregon Ave.
(541) 389-6116, facebook.com/ranchrecordsbend

WITNESS LOCAL ART AT ITS BEST
AT THE WORKHOUSE

Located next to The Sparrow Bakery (#12), The Workhouse hosts some of Bend's best local artisans. Since the 1920s when it housed a machine shop that fashioned the intricate pieces needed in the lumber mills, the old brick building has always been associated with artistic endeavors. Presently, a collective of several local artists uses the space as a studio for the creation of their eclectic mix of goods. Dozens of other artists contribute to the creative vibe with everything from postcards, T-shirts, and pillows to handmade soaps, jewelry, and monster piggy banks. Don't expect to find the cheap, imported merchandise so easily available in the conventional souvenir shops. If you want a unique, made-in-Bend souvenir that cannot be found anywhere else, The Workhouse should be your first stop.

50 SE Scott St., Ste. 6
(541) 241-2754, theworkhousebend.com

GET YOUR OUTDOOR GEAR
AT GEAR FIX

Bend is a city of adventure, full of people who respect and love the outdoors. The thing is, outdoor gear can be pricey, so smart shoppers want to get the best gear at the best price.

Go to Gear Fix. Located in the Box Factory, the store buys, sells, and trades most anything an outdoor enthusiast can imagine. Biking, skiing, hiking, climbing; if it's something used for an outside activity, chances are they have it. Plan to get rid of your old gear? They will try to sell it for you on consignment. And not only does Gear Fix sell clothing and equipment, they also can repair most anything, from the soles of your shoes to the helmet on your head!

550 SW Industrial Way, Ste. 183
(541) 617-0022, gearfix.com

SHINE LIKE THE SUN
AT THE SUNSTONE STORE

Walk into The Sunstone Store and you will be dazzled by the array of colors and amazed at the quality of handcrafted jewelry on display. Many states have an official gemstone, and Oregon has one of the most stunning. So desirable because of its distinctive glitter and shine, the sunstone can be found in shades of orange, gold, and red. Steven and Elyse Douglas, the owners of the Bend shop, have taken a gem which is already precious and molded it into something wearable that enhances whatever it adorns. The family is involved from the beginning to the end of the process. They mine the rocks by hand in Eastern Oregon, bring them back to Bend, and artfully use their skills to create unique pieces of handcrafted jewelry. Such attention and effort put into the craft deserve appreciation. If you want to shine like the sun, take home a piece of Oregon from The Sunstone Store.

920 NW Bond St., Ste. 106
(541) 389-2901, sunstonestore.com

LOAD UP ON ANTIQUES
IN REDMOND

Antique hunters, I haven't forgotten about you. Decades of elusive treasures await in Redmond. The two top shops, Farmer's Co-op Antiques and Redmond Antique Mall, are huge and have an amazing accumulation of everything imaginable. I'm not talking about junk here, I'm talking about high quality and often valuable items: furniture, books, china, coins, tools, toys, jewelry, military and farm equipment, typewriters, old phone booths—I could go on forever! Every nook and cranny in these shops is filled with something interesting and eye-catching. Going with my young daughters and explaining the uses of things from the past is an education in itself, and there is enough there to make a day of it.

Redmond Antique Mall, 2127 S Hwy 97
(541) 548-6208, facebook.com/Redmond-Antique-Mall

Farmer's Co-op Antiques, 106 SE Evergreen Ave., Ste. A
(541) 548-7975, facebook.com/redmondfarmerscoop

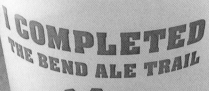

I COMPLETED
THE BEND ALE TRAIL

BENDALETRAIL.COM

 BEND ALE TRAIL

SUGGESTED
ITINERARIES

GETTING STARTED ON THE ALE TRAIL

Sip a Brew with a Sweet View at Bend Brewing Company, 13

Get a Hoppy Education on a Deschutes Brewery Tour, 25

Do Your Best Jack Nicholson Impression at Worthy Brewing, 10

Discover the Secret Rooms of McMenamins, 43

AN EVENING DOWNTOWN WITH ADULTS

Beware Los Luchadores at Barrio, 14

Fine Dine from A-Z in Bend, 21

Catch a Performance at Tower Theatre, 35

Relish Some Grown-Up Time at Velvet, 4

Sing Your Heart Out During Karaoke at Astro Lounge, 30

A DAY DOWNTOWN WITH KIDS

Stroll through Drake Park, 80

Fill Up on a Tasty Pizza Pie at Pizza Mondo, 22

Imagine a Trip to Italy at Bontà, 12

Satisfy Your Sweet Tooth at Cravin's, 9

Loiter in the Alleys of Downtown, 105

Savor the Best of Both Worlds at Dudley's Bookshop, 123

• •

A SHORT STAY IN BEND

Bond with Nature on the Deschutes River Trail, 60

Float or Paddleboard the Deschutes River, 74

Stand on Top of a Volcano at Pilot Butte State Park, 96

Do Your Best Jack Nicholson Impression at Worthy Brewing, 10

Revitalize in the Hot Pool at McMenamins, 44

Pick Up a Souvenir at One of These Shops, 124

Absorb the Sunset at Crux Fermentation, 19

FREE STUFF

Lose Yourself in the Forest at Shevlin Park, 58

Hear the Roar of the Mighty Rapids at Benham and Dillon Falls, 92

Bond with Nature on the Deschutes River Trail, 60

Drive the Picturesque Cascade Lakes Scenic Byway, 76

View the Cascades of Tumalo Falls, 83

Hear the Mighty Roar of Steelhead Falls, 68

Stroll through Drake Park, 80

Get Your Surf Up at Bend Whitewater Park, 73

Tour a Chocolate Factory at Goody's, 7

EXTREME FUN IN CENTRAL OREGON

Hike Misery Trail and Live to Tell about It, 86

Defy Death Bungee Jumping over the Crooked River, 99

Build Those Leg Muscles at Phil's Trailhead, 75

Trail Run through Archie Briggs Canyon, 84

OUTDOORS WITH THE KIDS

Photo courtesy of Toni Toreno
@BendPhotoTours

ACTIVITIES
BY SEASON

SPRING

SUMMER

• •

FALL

WINTER

Photo courtesy of Toni Toreno
@BendPhotoTours

INDEX

• •

• •

• •

• •

• •